ERIKA SEAMAYER-WILLIAMSON

AMAZING

Retreat Lifestyle

GRACE

Your journey to freedom

Your step-by-step guide to living...

The Amazing Grace Retreat Lifestyle

Acknowledgments

Book design by: Virginia "Ginny" Baker

Edited by: Shelley Jane McCullough

And

'my original artwork'

AMAZING
Retreat Lifestyle
GRACE
Your journey to freedom

Table of Contents

A personal note from Erika...

The purpose of this study is to help you find clarity, overcome struggles, and discover your true calling.
Also, to break through your fears or insecurities, finding true forgiveness; so that you can fulfill all that God wants you to be, do, and have in your life. When you truly understand the *Spiritual Gifts* that God has given you, your purpose will become clear.

It is my privilege to share my testimony of
what God has done in AND through my life.
I pray that during our time together,
you see a glimpse of God's greatness
and grow into a stronger relationship
with Jesus.

Ephesians 4:7 *But grace was given to each one of us according to the measure of Christ's gifts.*

Colossians 3:16 *Let the word of Christ dwell in you richly in all wisdom, teaching and admonishing one another in psalms and hymns and spiritual songs, singing with grace in your hearts to the Lord.*

Erika Seamayer-Williamson

Logo by Shadow Sky Creative Co.

AMAZING GRACE

Retreat Lifestyle
Your journey to freedom

Welcome to the Amazing Grace Retreat
Lifestyle Study

I am so grateful you have chosen to learn more about
"The Retreat Lifestyle"!
Go on this journey with me to reveal all that
God has planned for your life.
Take a moment to prepare your heart, to hear from the Holy Spirit with
an open mind, eyes, and ears, and to welcome
God's perfect peace.
If you have them, you may even want to select your favorite
Young Living Essential Oils, and start your diffuser now.
*My favorites for Prayer and Bible Studies are:
Three Wise Men, Envision, and Clarity.

Philippians 4: 6-7

*"Don't worry about anything; instead, pray about everything. Tell God
what you need, and thank him for all he has done. Then you will
experience God's peace, which exceeds anything we can understand. His
peace will guard your hearts and minds as you live in Christ Jesus."*

*"Be anxious for nothing, but in everything by prayer and supplication, with
thanksgiving, let your requests be made known to God; and the peace of
God, which surpasses all understanding, will guard your hearts and
minds through Christ Jesus."*

With Gratitude...

This study, Amazing Grace Talk Podcast, Amazing Grace Retreats, and The Book Ministry would not be possible without God's wonderful guidance. If I had not sought His will for my life, I wouldn't be where I am today. It is my heart's desire to love others and help teach them about God's love and Amazing Grace. When I read the *Prayer of Jabez by Bruce Wilkinson* in 2011 and began to pray this prayer every day, my life changed forever.

To my incredibly sweet, patient, and understanding husband, Erik. Who has believed in me through this journey and the dream God put in my heart to build this ministry to help others in their walk with Him. His love and encouragement are what keep me going.

To my daughter, Erika Laine, who has been with me every step of the way, serving faithfully alongside me growing up in church and all the Amazing Grace retreats since we began in 2016. We have been through many tough times but always kept our relationship with God front and center. I believe this is what has made our relationship so strong!

To my daddy, Rudy Seamayer, who was of German descent and graduated from this earth to Heaven on May 7, 2020, after a battle with Lewy Bodies Dementia. He was 89 years old. He always encouraged me and listened to my ideas with a smile. He taught me loyalty and to follow through. This book was launched on May 7, 2022, in memory of him. I miss you every day!

To my mom, Kay Seamayer, for modeling strength and determination, to be positive, and never give up. To run from negative people and share kindness with others.

To my Ginny. A friendship that began so long ago. You have taught me so much and I couldn't do this without you! Your love, support, and belief in me were sent straight from Heaven! Thank you for all you have done to make this book happen.

To ShelleyJane who has become the wind beneath my wings, in partnership, business, friendship and ministry. Love you!

I'm grateful for Fellowship Church in Downtown Dallas, TX. It was our home church for 12 years. For all of the amazing friendships, the lessons Erika Laine and I learned there were invaluable to our lives. Pastors Ed and Lisa Young showed us how to love and serve God so faithfully. One of my favorite memories during our time there was the day Erika Laine and I were also baptized when she was 12 years old. Erika Laine found her voice singing on the praise and worship team, and I believe this was crucial to her spiritual growth for all of these things, I am extremely thankful.

To our current church family at Trinity in Cedar Hill, TX. To each and every friend, prayer warrior, who has prayed over us and taught us so much, we love you and are so grateful to have you in our lives. As for Pastors Jim and Becky Hennesy, you have meant more to us than you will ever know! Thanks to our niece, Lyndsey for inviting us! We just KNEW this was the next step for our Spiritual Growth and the Lord's plans for our lives. Since then, God has taken us into the "deep waters" of our life and ministry. Erik and I have grown exponentially in our relationship with Jesus and are forever grateful.

To The Amazing Grace Prayer Team. Wow. I had no idea how much prayer and covering we would need to live out God's plans and purposes! The Amazing Grace Retreats, Podcast, the Book Ministry, and my everyday life. Many of you have been praying for this ministry faithfully. I'm so grateful for each one of you! You are ALL so important in helping us plant seeds to grow the Kingdom of Heaven. If you would like to be a part of our prayer team please reach out to us at www.theamazinggracelifestyle.com

I could write a book just on how grateful I am for all of my friends, family, sisters, Prayer Warriors, Spiritual Mentors, teachers, and preachers, who have been there for me. You know who you are! I want all of you to know how much I truly love and appreciate you from the bottom of my heart and carry your teaching with me every day.

I dedicate this book to our 4 children and 6 grandchildren. Your Dad and I are so proud of all of you!

Building Faith outside your Comfort-Zone

There is a **Google Calendar** and then there is **GOD's Calendar.**

For most people, normal has to do with a comfort zone, routine, control, and predictability. Normal feels good. But is normal always good for us?

It largely depends on our relationship with "normal". When normal becomes an expected or demanded prerequisite for living; it may not be serving our best interest and highest good...at least not personally. Discovering your Spiritual Gifts and leaning into God's ideas for your life can allow you to live the ULTIMATE LIFE, which I call the "Amazing Grace Retreat Lifestyle."

I honestly believe that the pain, trauma, and suffering I've been through was simply for me to learn from, make better decisions, and have a deeper relationship with the God of the Universe.

Cry out to Him, invite Him into your daily life, and you will be pleasantly surprised by not feeling alone or that you have to figure out everything on your own. In Proverbs 3:5-6 ,*"Trust in the Lord with all your heart and lean not on your own understanding."*
Jesus changes EVERYTHING!

Our comfort zones will keep us from our DESTINY.
So, don't be afraid! Let's go on this journey together! Begin to live the life you have always dreamed of. It happened to me!

Proverbs 16:3
"Commit your actions (ways) to the LORD, and your plans will succeed."

Hebrews 2:4 While God also bore witness by signs, wonders, various miracles, and gifts of the Holy Spirit distributed according to his will.

Jonah 2:8 *Those who worship false Gods, turn their backs on all God's mercies.*

Likewise, if you are stuck in an unwanted phase of your life, it may be because you are not listening to God. If you refuse to listen and obey Him, you may stay stuck! You need to be **willing** to get out of your comfort zone and obey His call on your life. If it is your desire for God to move in your life, you must take the first step. It breaks my heart when I see people allow FEAR to control their lives. Staying stuck in a miserable job, an unhealthy relationship, or an unproductive phase of life. Not that we don't all go through this from time to time. However, you can tell when someone continues on a path of unhappiness by not obeying and listening, as if their lives would be over if they failed! A failed attempt is how we learn perseverance and gain character to be ready for the next challenge.

God can use this to shine His light through you!
Then, we can teach others to learn and grow in God's ways. There are countless ways He speaks to us. He may give you an idea that suddenly solves a problem or situation. He may give you words that encourage or confirm another person's words. Many times God speaks to me first thing in the morning when I wake up, not audibly but through an idea or a thought. I have learned to write it down immediately so that, I don't forget these seeds of wisdom. Also, practice paying attention to signs, miracles, and wonders. If you wake up at a strange time, note the time and Google it. There might be a scripture associated with it. God **always** wants to speak to us. He may be wanting to tell you something through these signs.

To Forgive or not to Forgive...

This is a question asked by many at one time or another in life.
I remember years ago, I spoke these words, "Why should I forgive?"
They hurt me! They don't deserve it! Unfortunately, many people
have "stinking thinking." I'm sure I'm not the only one. When you
truly understand the "why" behind forgiveness, it will set you FREE! It
will bring you peace of mind and the freedom to enjoy the rest of
your life!

Even if you "think" you have forgiven, there is most likely work still to
do. If you hold any resentment, anger, or sadness. Or, you are just
simply stuck personally or professionally, year after year; there is
probably some unforgiveness somewhere that is
lurking in your subconscious and ultimately wreaking havoc
in your life.

Believe me, it's worth the "work" it takes to let go of the past and
get ready to move forward into God's plan and purpose, walking in
victory, not just surviving from day to day. And don't allow fear to
dictate your life! Let go and let God move.
Let's begin this journey together.
You will wish you had not wasted so many years holding on to
hurtful things. But, now you have the knowledge!

Matthew 6: 14-15
*If you forgive those who sin against you, your
Heavenly Father will forgive you. But if you refuse to forgive
others, your Father will not forgive your sins.*

How do we forgive?

- Acknowledge the hurt, pain, problem, or anger you feel about another person or a situation.
- Make this a Daily Practice. Each night, when you go to bed, ask yourself this question: "Have I put anyone outside my heart today?" Meaning, have I responded rudely to someone, or been impatient when I shouldn't have? Even something as small as saying something means when someone cuts you off in traffic. Or maybe something bigger. Did you lie to someone or cause someone harm? Get caught up in gossip? Or, did something happen so terrible that it changed the course of your life? Did it happen today or many years ago?
- Think of how easy it is to forgive a child who has done something they shouldn't have. Because of their innocence, it is easy for us to forgive them. Now think of that person...or yourself, the way you would forgive a small child. Then, forgive them and say it out loud. Forgive them for whatever they said or did and know that they were doing the best that they knew how to do.

Re-read this page as many times as you need to allow it to sink in, maybe even daily. Do you now see the danger that comes with not forgiving yourself or someone else who has hurt you?

Please DO NOT allow yourself to become *that* person who hangs on to the past their entire life with bitterness, anger, and resentment.

God is a God of healing and restoration.

Hebrews 12:15
"See to it that no one fails to obtain the grace of God; that no "root of bitterness" springs and causes trouble, and by it many become defiled."

Why should I let them off the hook?

Forgive them because it release us from the pain and brings FREEDOM to our lives! So, we can move on to our true purpose to live and walk in victory.

Where is justice?

The Cross of Jesus Christ makes forgiveness legally and
morally right.
Be careful to not rationalize the offender. Do not excuse them.
Also, forgiveness does not mean that it is necessary to establish
a relationship. Healthy boundaries are also necessary
for healing. You may never have a relationship with this person again, or it may be limited. Pray and allow God to guide you in these situations. Don't try and figure it out on your own. We were not meant to do life alone!

Take a minute to ask God in prayer...

Lord, search my heart. Is there someone I need to forgive?
Even if it is someone you think you have already forgiven;
write down the names of people or situations. Also, do not forget
about yourself. Sometimes, forgiving ourselves is the hardest thing to
do. There is nothing you have done in your life that is too big for God.
But, He wants you to recognize your mistakes and allow Him to wash
you clean. He is perfect in all His ways!

Shame and Guilt

When we hold on to those little issues of shame, bitterness, condemnation, judgment, and guilt, we stop God's blessings from flowing into our lives. Forgiving (even when we don't want to) opens a way for more good to flow into our lives. You may feel that you have a right to these feelings; the truth of the matter is...there is danger in not letting go. What we are really doing is building up a big wall around us so that no one can get through to us. **The GOOD that we desire and deserve cannot get in.** A lot of the time, I find that what is keeping someone from moving on in a happy relationship or a better more peaceful life is that they haven't forgiven someone or something in their past. Why do I know this?
Because it happened to me.

My forgiveness story set me free!

I was a single mom for 16 years. Sometimes I would date younger guys. I was cute and looked younger than I actually was so it just seemed to fit. After going through the *Road Adventure* and doing some deep healing emotional work, I realized that subconsciously, I had my guard up knowing full on that our relationship would never work out, because of their age. This allowed me to just have fun and not commit and then, THEY COULD'NT HURT ME!" Plus I was raising my daughter and she was my 1st priority. When I learned the truth about my choices, it changed my life forever!

I literally thought I had forgiven my ex-husband. But, the truth of the matter was, I had not. So, on my way home from the Road Adventure that night, I thought, "What do I have to lose?" I was in my car by myself and I spoke the words out loud. Actually, I was screaming out the words from all the hurt and pain! I forgive you for_____!____!___!
I was screaming out every offense that came to my mind, and tears were running down my face. My voice did not sound like my own, but more like an evil yucky voice, seriously. I'm not trying to scare anyone, but I had been hanging on to so much hurt, anger, and resentment for so long that it had taken up roots in me. This was my second experience walking through deliverance. If you are unfamiliar with this word, here is the meaning.

The act of delivering someone or something: the state of being delivered, especially liberation or rescue. It is the action of beingrescued or set free. I want to tell you that my life was changed forever by this simple act. When you surrender all in prayer, it activates God's blessings. That is the only way I know to describe it. I almost felt as if it had never happened. Oh yes, the memories are still there. But be careful not to repeat these stories just for the sake of repeating them. It will put you directly back into that emotional state and can be very draining. You will know if God is using your story for His glory.

One of the most important things I ever learned about unforgiveness...

You may be holding onto something that tore you apart, wrecked your world, or caused you so much pain that it keeps you from moving into all of God's gifts that He has for you. Remember, "they" may not even know how much they hurt you or even care. And, you are spending valuable time holding on to something that the offender did to you. You may be thinking, "I can't believe they would do this or that?". So forgive and avoid wasting time. It's not hurting them, only you! Move into the blessings that God has for you. Seriously!

We all know the horrific story of Elizabeth Smart, right?
The quote from Elizabeth's Mom was one of the best pieces of advice I've ever heard. She said, "Elizabeth, what these people have done to you is terrible, and there are no words strong enough to describe how wicked and evil they are," They have stolen nine months of your life from you that you will *never* get back. But the best punishment you could ever give them is to be happy, to move forward with your life, to do all the things you want to do. By feeling sorry for yourself, by holding onto the past, by reliving it; that is only allowing them to steal more of your life away from you. And they don't deserve that, and they don't deserve a single second more. So you need to be happy and you need to move on with your life." If Elizabeth can accomplish forgiveness for what happened to her, anyone can.

Scriptures on Forgiveness

It's natural to think...someone should pay for my pain.

I promise if you let go and surrender...HE will take care of it and walk you through it with Grace and Love. Here are some scriptures to pray, meditate and journal.

Psalm 32:1-2 *"Oh, what a joy for those whose disobedience is forgiven, whose sin is put out of sight!"*

Psalm 32:5 *"Finally, I confessed all of my sins to you and stopped trying to hide my guilt. I said to myself, I will confess my rebellion to the LORD. And you forgave me! All my guilt is gone."*

Luke 6:37 *"Do not judge others, and you will not be judged. Do not condemn others, or it will all come back against you. Forgive others, and you will be forgiven."*

Colossians 3:13-15 *"Make allowance for each other's faults and forgive anyone who offends you. Remember, the Lord forgave you, so you must forgive others. 14 Above all, clothe yourselves with love, which binds us all together in perfect harmony. 15 And let the peace that comes from Christ rule in your hearts. As members of one body, you are called to live in peace. And, always be thankful."*

*On the next two FORGIVENESS pages, write out who you want to forgive...a person, a hurtful situation, or maybe even yourself. Then, surrender this to God. Also write them on an index card so you can burn or tear them up, bury or throw them away! "Let it go!" God already has! Then you will be set FREE to move forward and live without this on your mind.

FORGIVE

FORGIVE

HEALTHY
Boundaries

Healthy boundaries are a reflection of the principles, expectations, and guidelines that you have set for yourself. The fact is, you may not even be aware. Most people are not. When those boundaries are broken with disrespect, emotional manipulation usually begins. This can happen even with the best of friends or family. It is important to learn how to speak up for yourself and know your worth. Practice saying, "I'd love to but I won't be able to help you this time. You will feel the need to, but practice not explaining yourself. The more you practice, the easier it becomes, and the sooner you will be set free from this form of bondage. Yes, I said bondage. I started to learn this practice when I was 30 years old. I felt sick many times because "friends" were taking advantage of me and my time. There is so much FREEDOM in saying NO, and you will gain back your worth and self-dignity. Your life matters to God, and it should matter to you!
Codependent No More, by Melody Beattie.
And remember...
People only treat you the way you allow them to! Ouch, right?

IT'S OKAY TO SAY NO

When I was divorced, my ex-husband would try and control me by interrupting my weekend and the plans I had made with friends by demanding that he drop her off early when he knew I was at the lake and not close to home. Or call the house phone after our daughter's bedtime, which was very disruptive. I told him that he could call anytime after school up until bedtime, which was 8:00. Inevitably, he would call after that time. So I started unplugging the phone at 8:00, and guess what? Our home was once again peaceful, and we could stay on schedule. And another thing, if your X is bothering or harassing you through text, block them and only allow emails. This way, you won't be on an emotional roller coaster throughout your day. And I promise you, if there is an emergency, you will know. Do not be manipulated and feel guilty just because you have kids together. You are divorced for a reason.

On this page, you can practice saying no. Create four friendly phrases that reflect a rejection of an invitation or request. For example, Thank you for thinking of me, but I will not be able to make it or help you. Maybe next time. :)

Saying no will become natural when you practice out loud. It is imperative that you value your time and the purposes that God has placed on your life rather than putting others before yourself. This is a hard truth that someone shared with me many years ago, and it changed my life. So honor yourself and your time.

_____

_____

_____

_____

_____

_____

_____

_____

_____

_____

_____

_____

_____

Roadmap to the Retreat Lifestyle

Morning Routine- Develop a specific time every day to spend with God. I started getting up at 5 am many years ago after reading the book, *Secrets of the Vine,* by Bruce Wilkinson. This is when I pray, journal, read my Bible, or sit quietly, meditating on HIS words and promises. There's something about getting up before your household to start your day. This has brought me so much peace and harmony. I challenge you to try it, set your alarm for 15 minutes earlier and see how you feel. I'll bet your anxiety and stress levels lighten and you will go through your day with more joy!

Exercise- Choose some type of exercise that you enjoy. My favorites are tennis, Yoga Faith (don't be scared, Yoga is a practice, not a religion), walking, or hiking. And I love ballet, being in my 50's, it isn't easy, but stretching is so good for the body! We must keep moving. (I'm preaching to myself) ha

Lunch or Dinner Date- Plan a date with a friend and put it in your calendar. I love fancy! So, the *Zodiac Room* at Neiman Marcus is one of my favorites. Or, just get together at your home or a friend's home. The importance here is to make time for your friendships. *If you are married, put your spouse first. In God's eyes, this is the most important relationship next to your relationship with Jesus. Keeping a Date Night is so important, especially when you have children at home.*

A Spa Day- Plan a Spa Day for yourself! You can get a service or a full day. Enjoy lunch, a hot tub, a sauna, and whatever else they have to offer. My favorites here in Dallas are *The Spa at The Crescent*, or *The Spa at the Adolphus*. You can also book a monthly pedicure or a reflexology appointment. Those are budget-friendly and so relaxing. Treat yourself! You are worth it!

Roadmap to the Retreat Lifestyle

Vacations- Plan a get-a-way for yourself. Everyone needs time away to refresh and recharge. Any length of vacation is good! You can go on a weekend getaway or a camping trip. Another idea would be a night's stay at a Bed-and-Breakfast. It's important to spend time away from your home, work and responsibilities.

Natural Remedies First- I started using Young Living ❀ Essential Oils many years ago. I wish I had known about them sooner. Since then, I have used Essential Oils for emotional healing, physical improvement, prayer time, and cleaning my home without harmful toxins. It could be life-changing for you as it was for our family. Raindrop technique is also amazing for relaxing and healing.

Organization- Having an organized home and workspace helps your mental clarity and overall health. When you de-clutter your space and find effective and beautiful ways to organize; you feel a sense of accomplishment. You can start with one room or a small area. It is life-changing. Check out https://thehomeedit.com for great ideas.

Family Time- Making your family a priority is so important. Remember, this is your legacy. Whether it's Holiday Gatherings or a Birthday Date; schedule it and make them feel special!

Healthy Mindset- Stay focused on positive/healthy relationships. It is very important to be intentional about what you watch, read, and listen to. Speaking positive affirmations over yourself as if God is speaking to you. YOU are a child of God and extremely VALUABLE! Or, sign up for *The Road Adventure*, or *Fellowship of the Sword*, it advanced me 10 years ahead in my personal relationship with God and it will you too!

Church Family- Find a place of worship that meets your needs. You can quickly meet like-minded people for corporate worship, teachings, friendship, and prayer. We were not meant to "do life" alone.

Volunteering-When you volunteer at your local church or favorite charity, you begin to discover your God-given talents and purpose in life. You set out to serve God; but in return, you gain more than you could ever imagine. Try it...I can't wait to hear all about how God blesses YOU through serving! The best advice a friend gave me many years ago when I was at my lowest was to go and help someone else. And, you will forget about your problems! God will take care of you!

Side note: If you would like to volunteer for our non-profit, Amazing Grace Ministries, bringing hope and healing to Single Mothers and their children, in crises situations. We help "bridge the gap" by providing support, a Healing Process, and guidance through Biblical Principles. Please go to www.thamazinggracelifestyle.com

Spiritual Gifts

In His grace, God has given us different gifts for doing certain things well.
Romans 12:6

Serving

Rendering practical help in both physical and spiritual matters.

Pastor

Leading, overseeing, training, and caring for the needs of a group of Christians.

Prophecy

The giving of encouragement and affirmation.

Mercy

Identifying with and comforting those who are in distress. The ability to show empathy with them, not just for them.

Teaching

Communicating knowledge and making known the facts of Scripture.

Administration

Organizing, administering, promoting & leading various affairs of the Church.

Spiritual Gifts

Where do you see yourself? Don't overthink it.
Go with your first instinct.
Or, you can take a quick test here: www.focusonthefamily.com

Mercy

Pastor

Prophecy

Serving

Teaching

Administration

The Prayer of Jabez
a few helpful scriptures

1 CHRONICLES 4:10 "And, Jabez called on the God of Israel saying, "Oh, that You would bless me indeed, and enlarge my territory, that Your hand would be with me, and that You would keep me from evil, that I may not cause pain!" So God granted him what he requested."

Matthew 7:7-8 "Ask, and it will be given to you; seek, and you will find; knock, and it will be opened to you. For everyone who asks receives, and he who seeks finds, and to him who knocks it will be opened."

Psalm 119:18 "Open my eyes, that I may see wondrous things from Your law."

"O LORD, ENLARGE MY BORDERS!"
Expect great things from God; attempt great things for God.
Why should I ask God for more territory? We wonder.
I can't keep up with my life now!

God will arrange *circumstances* and *opportunities* that are more strategic for you. It will be as if God has become your master scheduler.

You won't get more hours in the day, but you will discover more effective ways of using the hours you're given.
The Holy Spirit will show you the way.

As you start to understand this, you will notice that some of your borders will extend in certain areas of your life, and other borders will shrink. Things that mattered before will drop off your priority list when we surrender all and ask for God's help.

Stop and think for a minute or two...What are some opportunities you may have missed? For instance, maybe there's a job promotion that you could apply for. Maybe you have dreamed of a career change or start something new? Maybe you want to volunteer for something that you are passionate about? How will you know if you don't take a step? Pray about it and then listen. God will answer you. He wants His will in your life! But pay attention to how he answers. Don't be one of those people who say, I'm waiting on God to tell me. The fact is, He probably already has and you are still allowing *fear* to stop you from moving forward. Yes, God knows your heart and knows all of your desires and needs, but we have to ask. When we ask, He responds.

- Ask yourself: What am I passionate about? What comes easy for me? What do you wake up thinking about? What do others ask me to do, sing, decorate, help? Don't overthink it...it will come to you. Write it down and ask the Lord how to take the next step.

For example: It's easy for me to talk with people and connect with them. Listening is a skill I consciously practice. You are naturally better at one or the other, but you can learn how to be better communicators. When I was in school, I always got in trouble for talking! Now, I have a podcast (Amazing Grace Talk), I'm a Speaker, and a Life Coach (Amazing Grace Lifestyle Coaching). I'm always talking!

We all have natural abilities and talents to live in our purpose. Now it's your turn to learn your gifts. And, you can use them to bless others and have a fulfilled life.

Facing Your Fears

2 TIMOTHY 1:7 God has not given us a spirit of fear, but of power and of love, and of a sound mind.

JOSHUA 1:9 Have I not commanded you? Be strong and of good courage; Do not be afraid, nor be dismayed, for the LORD your God is with you wherever you go.

Ask yourself these important questions and be honest with yourself:

- What specific *FEAR* is keeping me from being bold for God and living out my dreams?

- What is the worst thing that could happen if I stepped out in faith?

- On the other hand, what good things could happen?

- Or, what else could be stopping you?

- What are some of the lies you believe? Are they giving power to your fears? The next time you face that fear, what should you do?

Keep Christ first in your thoughts and actions; press ahead toward God's plans for your life. And, let the past go!

When God calls you to a larger plan for Him and you respond; He has a prize in mind. Go for the prize, my friend, until you draw your last breath.

Until the moment you step into eternity, you'll never fully know the dimensions of His generous love and important purpose for you!

EXODUS 33:19 Could God be that good? And the Lord said, "I will cause my goodness to pass in front of you, and I will proclaim my name, the Lord, in your presence.

MALACHI 3:10 Bring all the tithes into the storehouse, That there may be food in My house, And try Me now in this," Says the Lord of hosts, "If I will not open for you the windows of heaven and pour out for you such blessing. That there will not be room enough to receive it.

HELLO
my name is

What are some names you call yourself?

Ask yourself, what do you speak over your life? Do
you judge yourself? What names have you been called
and taken in as your identity? Disappointment, stupid, a mistake,
unwanted, failure, rejection, not pretty enough, not skinny enough, not
tan enough, too short, too tall?!

God had more in store for Jabez than pain. And, He has more in store
for you, too! He won't ask you to ignore or deny a difficult past or limiting
circumstances. But he'll **never** define you by it. Your Father's name for
you isn't pain or any such word.

These are HIS names for you...
CHOSEN, ROYAL, HOLY, SPECIAL, and His BELOVED!
1 Peter 2:9 But you are a *chosen* generation, a royal priesthood, a holy
nation, His own special people, that you may proclaim the praises of Him
who called you out of darkness into His marvelous light;
Song of Solomon 6:3 I am my beloved's, And my beloved is *mine*. He
feeds his flock among the lilies.
Isaiah 62:12 And they shall call them The Holy People, The Redeemed
of the Lord; And you shall be called Sought Out, A City Not Forsaken.

GOD LOVES NOBODIES

*Have you noticed that Jesus was unusually attracted to people
who had emptiness in their lives? Those labeled losers, loners, the sick,
the lame, the weak, and the DESPERATE. These were
the ones He came for! He met all their needs!

The Secret of Abundance

PSALM 37:3-4 Trust in the Lord, and do good; dwell in the land, and feed on His faithfulness. Delight yourself also in the Lord, and He shall give you the desires of your heart.

- Trust God enough to ask for what you want! Bring all your requests- spiritual, emotional, and material- to God in prayer.

- Once trust takes root in your heart, you are ready to take the next bold step into the blessed life. Remember, abundance is not always about finances. When people hear peace in your voice and see your actions of love and grace for others, then and only then will they see Jesus in YOU! God makes a way for things to happen even when they appear as if there was no way!

- The secret of true abundance in your life is to want what God wants for you.

When you pray: Ask God, what are 2 or 3 things that YOU want for me? Then wait. Let Him "download" an idea or thought in your heart and mind. Sometimes the answer comes right away and sometimes we already know. It is just important to speak it out loud and come into agreement with our creator.

What happens when you take this prayer to heart? Well, this is what Bruce Wilkinson (the author of the book) calls your "Jabez Appointments". and you don't want to miss any! So, if you start praying this prayer, get ready for the ride of your life! Is it easy? No, but living for God is the best feeling in the world, and if you trust him and continue to ask Him; He will be your compass.
If you're facing a mountain today, there's a good chance that you're in the right place. A place where God's supernatural power can be released for His Glory.

To this day, it is so much fun to hear others' "Jabez Stories." Including Erik, my sweet husband, and many close friends whom I have discovered pray this prayer too!

My "Jabez" story...

After reading the book, *The Prayer of Jabez*,
I began praying this prayer every day.
I was surprised to find that people were basically coming out of
NOWHERE sharing their stories with me. Things I had grown through...
like unforgiveness and codependency.

As I began to listen and respond with an open heart, many would tear
up within just a few minutes of the conversation. Saying things like, "I
have never thought of 'it' that way". First, it was one or two people a
week, then grew to three and four people a week. I didn't know what
to think! Then, I shared this with an elderly lady. She said, "Honey,
you don't know what that is? " I said, "No, but you look like YOU do, so
can you tell me?" She said God has gifted you with the Spirit of
Discernment. I knew the definition but did not understand what it
meant for me. So, I went home and prayed for it. And, then I
understood that this was one of my Spiritual Gifts.

Lifting and building up others to show them God's love and grace!
Making beauty out of ashes. Suddenly, all the TERRIBLE things that I
had gone through were for a purpose! To encourage others and show
them that they didn't have to stay stuck in a life that was not serving
them or anyone else.

As Pastor Ed Young always says,
"God is preparing YOU for what He has prepared FOR you!"
These were words that I
hung on to when I was going through the WORST and hardest times
of my life. It is what gave me hope.

24

Goals
Ask and you shall receive

Numbers 24:4 The utterance of him who hears the words of God, Who sees the *vision* of the Almighty, who falls down, with eyes wide open:

Habakkuk 2:2 The just live by faith then the Lord answered me and said: "Write the *vision* And make it plain on tablets, that he may run who reads it.

Proverbs 16:9 A man's heart plans his way, but the Lord directs his steps.

Proverbs 21:5 The plans of the diligent lead surely to plenty, but those of who are hasty, surely to poverty.

Proverbs 19:21 There are many plans in a man's heart, nevertheless the Lord's counsel—that will stand.

Philippians 3:14 I press toward the goal for the prize of the upward call of God in Christ Jesus.

Goals continued...

If you have a DREAM beyond your financial means or your ability, this will require your faith and His supernatural provision. Here are a few questions that will get your mind thinking...

1. What would you do if there were no limits?

2. What would it look like?

3. If your life were perfect what would it look like?
   - Income
   - Family
   - Health
   - Net Worth
   - Spiritual Walk

4. What things in your life would you like to change most?

5. What are you most passionate about and why?

6. What do you feel is holding you back from living your best life?

7. Do you make decisions based on your circumstances, thoughts, fears, and worries? Or, do you ask God first?

Goals continued…

Take the next 30 seconds and write down 3 of your most important goals or dreams. You will be surprised at how quickly you write them down. It must be clear, specific, & measurable!

1.

2.

3.

Goals continued...

What changes do you need to make
to accomplish each one of these goals?
Take positive action toward each goal
one step at a time.

- Set a goal end date

- Make a plan of action. What is your FIRST step? Don't
be afraid.....jump!

Goals continued...

Practice visualizing or "seeing" your goals.
Create clear, exciting, pictures of your goals as if they were already a reality.

Vision/Dream Board

This is my favorite! Get a corkboard or a foam core board. Cut out pics from a magazine or google a pic of something you have been dreaming of and print it. Or, cut out scriptures or sayings that inspire you! I love to update these. Do this with a friend, child, or spouse. Put it in a place that you look at every day! My Dream Board is in my office. I update it every 6 months to a year. I also will move things that have come to pass over to an accomplished board! Just have fun. Remember, just like the "Prayer of Jabez," God wants to give you all that you desire. All you have to do is ask and believe!

Vision Scriptures

"Where there is no vision the
people perish."
Proverbs 29:18

And the LORD answered me: "Write the vision; make it plain on
tablets, so he may run who reads it."
Habakkuk 2:2

"Delight yourself also in the Lord, and He shall give
you the desires of your heart.
Commit your way to the Lord, trust also in Him,
And He shall bring it to pass."
Psalm 37:4-5

"For I know the plans I have for you declares the Lord, plans to
prosper you and not to harm you, plans to give you hope and a
future."
Jeremiah 29:11

He said, "Listen to my words: When there is a prophet among
you, I, the LORD, reveal myself to them in visions,
I speak to them in dreams."
Numbers 12:6

"In the morning, LORD, you hear my voice; in the morning I lay my
requests before you and wait expectantly."
Psalm 5:3

Erika's Movie Recommendations...

The War Room

The Shack

The Passion of the Christ

The Son of God

Do you Believe?

Same Kind of Different as Me

Fireproof

The Chosen (series)

Erika's Retreat Recommendations...

Amazing Grace Retreats

The Road Adventure

Fellowship of the Sword

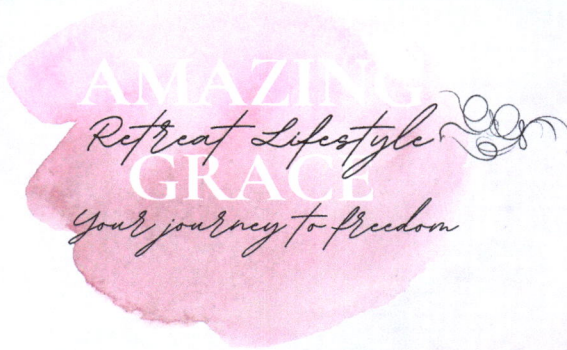

Erika's Book Recommendations...

The Prayer of Jabez, The Secrets of the Vine
The Dream Giver, all by **Bruce Wilkinson**

Draw the Circle, The 40-Day Prayer Challenge
by **Mark Batterson**

Fervent, by **Priscilla Shirer**

The Richest Man Who Ever Lived, The Greatest Words Ever Spoken,
Jesus Speaks, and The JOSEPH Principles
all by **Steven K Scott**

BORN to be FREE by Tom Vermillion

Healing Oils of the Bible, by David Stewart, Ph. D.

BeautyF U L L by Ed. Young and Mac Richard

Jesus Calling Daily Devotional By Sarah Young

BREAKING the Cycle of Offense by Dr. Larry Ollison

Codependent No More and The Language of Letting Go
by Mealody Beattie

My Story -
Erika Seamayer-Williamson

Growing up, I always remember believing in God. I never had a reason not to. I prayed at night and called on Him when I was in trouble. Ha!

When I was 24 years old, I started a job at a salon in Arlington called Hair Logics in Lincoln Square. I was told that it was a Christian Salon. What was the difference in other salons? Everyone who worked in the salon believed in God; all of them had a home church. We also prayed before our monthly meetings.

The owner of the salon became one of my first Spiritual Mentors. I started going to her church, it was a non-denominational Bible Church. I grew up in a church, singing the same ole songs every weekend. No disrespect, but I had never felt this inspired at church before. The music was moving my spirit in a way that I had never experienced & was learning and understanding the Bible in a whole new way. The messages were making sense in ways that I could apply in my everyday life.

At the salon, I was hearing how God was moving in people's lives as I had never heard before. One of my clients, Beth Ann, became another Christian mentor. When the student is ready, the teacher appears right? She taught me how to pray "specific prayers". This was such an eye-opener! And, I began this practice. And, my life changed!

Darlene, the owner of the salon, told me her miracle story about tithing. She knew the bible taught to give 10% of your income (and she didn't know how she could, but wanted to be obedient). She began to tithe to her church and God showed up through a client with a $10,000 check! This was the exact amount she needed to open her DREAM SALON! This is also where I had my first real God encounter and spiritual awakening of healing. After that, I was hooked! I was so grateful for this because my marriage was falling apart. At the time, I was married to my high school boyfriend.

34

We had dated for 6 years and then were married for 6 years. Our marriage was sort of bipolar. We were deeply in love with each other, but there was one problem; he was a binge drinker and occasional drug user. It was a very unsettling and abusive relationship at times. I was very codependent. But, at the time, I had no idea what that meant. Someone told me about the book, *Co-dependent no More*. I actually bought it to give to one of my clients but as I opened it to see what it was all about, tears began to fall! And, I realized this book is for me!!!

Clinging to my relationship with God and so desperate to learn how to live HIS way; I soon got out of my abusive marriage. I finally realized that I did not have the power to fix or change him. Only God does...and he had to make the decision to get help for himself.

After being a single mom for 16 years, I reconnected with my 5th-grade boyfriend, Erik. This was 22 years after we graduated high school. My daughter, Erika Laine, and I were living in Spearfish, South Dakota. He found me on Facebook and we were engaged in one week and married in 3 months in Cozumel, Mexico. I know that sounds crazy, all I can say is it wasn't and made perfect sense. We knew each other our whole lives and where we came from.

I had never experienced this kind of LOVE before. Such FREEDOM. We had a long-distance marriage from Aug 5, 2011, till around March of 2012 since Erika Laine was a senior at Sturgis High School. He would fly from Dallas to South Dakota about every 10 days. Then, Erika Laine and I went to Dallas for Christmas! After she graduated, we moved back to Texas. I have to say, as much as I wanted to be with my husband, family, and friends; I really did not want to move from South Dakota. I loved it there. The first year I was home was really a struggle. I was happier than I've ever been in my life relationally, but geographically I was miserable. I despise the heat of Texas summers. And, I love the mountains and the cooler weather & snow that I had found in South Dakota. Also, we had developed such great friendships there, so much so, that I call Spearfish HOME. Thankfully, my husband loves it there too, so we go back about every 3 months and plan to buy a vacation home to live there part-time one day!

On one of the visits, we stayed at a bed-and-breakfast of a friend. We were walking out, and I noticed this cute little book. It was *The Prayer of Jabez*. So, I stole it! LOL. No, not really. I text my friend that I had the book and wanted to read it and would mail it back to her. She said no, please keep it, enjoy it, or pass it on to someone else after you read it.

So, I brought it back to Texas and read it. This book spoke to me in such a way that was life-changing. That year, Bruce Wilkinson (the author of the book), became my favorite author. I then read *The Secrets of the Vine* and *The Dream Giver*. Wow, these were all life-changing books for me! And, I have been sharing them with people ever since. They are touching lives as they did for me. While in Texas, I tried to focus on things I could be happy about. My family, friends, and my home church were all dear to my heart because they gave me the foundation to grow my spiritual journey. Our pastor at that time was Ed Young. He is an amazing communicator. During the toughest times of my life, I clung to something that he always said, "God is preparing you for what He has prepared for you". And sure enough, it came true. All in God's perfect timing.

We joined the Country Club where I had grown up and I started playing tennis again for the first time in years. I played all through junior high and high school and was on the traveling team. Through the years, I had only coached at some tennis summer camps but never played on any teams since I was in high school. My husband is a golfer. So, this was a good choice for both of us.

During this time, I really dove into spending a lot of time with God. Our church offered a program called UNL (University of Next Level), which was a leadership school. So, I took several semesters of classes there. I had always admired people who would journal and spend daily time with God. But, I never could find the time or get into the discipline. God always knows what He is doing, even when we feel like we are lost. I look back now and realize how precious this time was to begin my journey. I began to have a much closer relationship with Him and realized how to live out my purpose in serving others.

Now, it is my daily prayer, hope, and privilege to help each and every person to hear from God so that they can have peace, joy, love ♥ and acceptance from our Lord and Savior.

Inviting you to follow me

@erikaseamayerwilliamson

For more information, please go to:

www.erikaseamayerwilliamson.com

Be "in the know" of all upcoming events by signing up for my email list.

Don't forget to check out the **Amazing Grace Talk Podcast** on Apple, Spotify, YouTube and Audible.

*All watercolor paintings in this book are my original artwork. I began painting after my Dad passed away on May 7, 2020, as a way to work through my grief. I feel that, "They may not be the most professional paintings, but with every brushstroke came healing." Find what soothes your soul and do it! If you would like to purchase any of them you can shop on my website above on the Shop page. The money goes toward our non-profit Amazing Grace Ministries.

These bears remind me of my Daddy, and Estes Park, Colorado where we used to take family trips each summer.

www.ingramcontent.com/pod-product-compliance
Lightning Source LLC
Chambersburg PA
CBHW041523090426
42737CB00037B/20